It's Raining

Nancy Hicer

Rosen REAL READERS

Rosen Classroom™
New York

Most water on the earth is
in rivers, lakes, and oceans.

The sun heats the water on the earth.

Water changes to gas
when it heats up.
It rises
into the sky.

Gas cools as it rises.
It turns into
small drops of water.
The drops stick together
and make clouds.

When water drops are too heavy,
they fall from a cloud.
Rain is water that
falls from clouds.

Rain falls onto the ground.
This is good for grass.
Rain helps
make grass green.

Plants need water.
They get most of it
from rain.

Rain fills lakes and rivers.
Animals drink this water.

Rain fills oceans.
Oceans hold most of
the earth's water.

After it rains
you can see a rainbow.
It has seven colors.

Words to Know

cloud

gas

grass

plant

rain

rainbow